LONDON'S BUSES
THE COLOURFUL ERA
1985–2005

MALCOLM BATTEN

AMBERLEY

First published 2018

Amberley Publishing
The Hill, Stroud
Gloucestershire, GL5 4EP

www.amberley-books.com

Copyright © Malcolm Batten, 2018

The right of Malcolm Batten to be identified
as the Author of this work has been asserted in
accordance with the Copyrights, Designs and
Patents Act 1988.

ISBN 978 1 4456 8403 1 (print)
ISBN 978 1 4456 8404 8 (ebook)

British Library Cataloguing in Publication Data.
A catalogue record for this book is available from
the British Library.

Orgination by Amberley Publishing.
Printed in the UK.

Contents

Introduction

From its establishment in 1933 until its demise in 1984, London Transport had monopoly powers, so only they ran buses within the Greater London area; although, actually, this wasn't quite true. There were a few services that came into London from outside the LT area that used buses: Eastern National had routes from Southend to Romford, Wood Green (Walthamstow from 1981) and King's Cross or Victoria; Thames Valley had run double-deckers from Reading to Victoria coach station; and their successor, Alder Valley, later used some double-deckers on the Reading and Bracknell–London services. In such cases there would usually be restrictions on carrying passengers wholly within the LT area.

London Transport had developed a network of limited-stop routes running under the Green Line brand, mainly linking towns at the outer limits of the country area by through routes across London. In 1970 London Transport had been split with the London Transport red buses and the Underground coming under the control of the Greater London Council, while the country green buses and Green Line services transferred to the National Bus Company as a new company – London Country Bus Services. In the 1970s the Green Line services were revised. Many traditional routes were withdrawn and new services were introduced to serve the airports or for commuters. London Country would be split into four parts in 1986 and each of these then took a different approach to Green Line operations. There was also an overlap between the old LT 'red' and 'green' areas, so LCBS and its successors had routes coming into the Greater London area. Similarly, London Transport had 'red' routes that ran out into the country beyond the Greater London Council area.

After the deregulation of long-distance journeys over 30 miles in 1980, Reading and Southend Corporations had started a joint service between their two towns, but this only lasted until 1982, when they decided to end the joint operation and develop their own services to London. Southend would become part of Arriva in 1998, while Reading ended their London service in 2000.

In 1982 the Greater London Council's decision to increase rates to subsidise the buses and Underground and encourage people to use these rather than private transport, the so-called 'Fares Fair' policy, was ruled illegal after a court challenge by Bromley Council. This resulted in fares being doubled, service cuts of 15 per cent, including withdrawal from country areas outside the GLC area, garage closures, and also the first withdrawals of Routemasters. The LT total bus fleet was reduced by some 600 vehicles.

The Conservative Government resolved to abolish the GLC, but London's transport could not just be handed over to the separate London boroughs. So the London Regional Transport Act (1984) was passed. From midnight on 29 June 1984, London Regional Transport took over from the GLC and London Transport ceased to exist. Then, from 1 April 1985, a new wholly owned subsidiary, London Buses Ltd, took on the operation of buses, with other subsidiaries for the Underground, the new Docklands Light Railway and Bus Engineering Ltd for bus maintenance.

The LRT Act also gave powers to seek competitive tenders for London's bus services. Nationally under the 1985 Transport Act the old system of bus route licensing was replaced by allowing open competition on commercially registered routes and competitive tendering elsewhere. London was spared competition at the time but LRT was required to put its routes out to competitive tender. The first round of these in July saw some routes retained by London Buses, while some passed to National Bus Company fleets on the fringe of the LT area – namely, Eastern National and London Country. Two other routes passed to existing coach operators. At first, many of the tendered routes were those on the outer edges of the LRT area, or were selected because of their small scale and the existence of independent operators nearby who were expected to bid for them. The third round of tendering in 1985 saw a whole area in Orpington being put to tender following a review of the existing network. This included not only existing LT routes but also those of London Country and existing independent operators Crystals and Metrobus. In subsequent years Central London routes were tendered and a whole range of companies from near and far were tempted to try their hand at the tendering process. Some proved to be more successful than others! Vehicles working on LRT tenders were required to carry the LRT logo, but companies could choose their own colour scheme and fleetname. Sometimes new vehicles would be bought for the routes, at other times second-hand vehicles would be used, including in many cases ex-London Daimler Fleetlines, which were being sold off after less than ten years in use. However, in mid-1989 LRT started specifying that buses on contract routes should not be more than seven years old, so new vehicles became the norm for new tenders and for upgrading existing ones.

Sometimes, the intended new vehicles were not delivered in time for the take-up of a route, in which case the operator would resort to hiring in vehicles from other bus companies, providing even more variety for London bus enthusiasts and bemusement to passengers. It also brought operational difficulties for the companies, as these might be types which the garage fitters were not familiar with.

Private companies were often able to put in lower bids than London Buses and win tendered contracts because their wage costs were lower than the highly unionised London Buses. Also, some were based outside the Greater London area, where housing costs might be lower. London Buses set up a number of local 'low cost' units with different staff and wage agreements to compete with other operators in the tendering process. These were mostly in the outer areas of the Greater London area, such as Potters Bar, Bexleyheath etc., where it was considered that living costs were lower than Central London. Some of these units used the standard London red livery with just a local fleetname, but in other instances – e.g. with Bexleybus in Bexleyheath and Roundabout at Orpington – a different livery was chosen, and these are included within.

There were also a few cases where private operators had already been working local bus routes wholly within the LT monopoly area, but you had to know where to look for them. These were either routes that had formerly been worked by London Transport and subsequently withdrawn, or in places where LT had not considered it worthwhile starting a service. Many of these services continued beyond the tendering process. In some cases, as with Metrobus, the company became a tendered bus operator and incorporated the route(s) into their network. However, in some other cases, the routings were covered by new tendered routes and passed to different operators.

When London Buses was divided into operating units in 1989, they adopted the standard livery style that had been agreed in 1988 with a grey skirt and thin white band, although some adaptation of this standard livery was allowed.

In 1990 there began to be a disagreement between the thinking of LRT and London Buses. LRT wanted all buses running tendered services under its authority to be in a common livery – i.e. red. London Buses did not want this as they felt that if people were to complain about a bus service they would be blamed, even if it was another company that was running the offending service. In the event other operators were allowed to keep their own liveries (for now at least), but London Buses companies had to be red. This meant the end for the Bexleybus blue and cream.

In the years after 1985 there was much speculation as to when (or if) London was to become fully deregulated and bus services opened up to full competition as elsewhere in the country. However in 1993 the then Transport Secretary John MacGregor unexpectedly made an announcement in which he stated '… while bus deregulation remains the long-term aim for London, the Government no longer intends to bring forward legislation in this Parliament to deregulate London's bus services.' However, the London Buses subsidiaries would be privatised, which then took place between January 1994 and January 1995. It was the intention that no one purchaser should be able to buy adjacent operating districts. In fact, Stagecoach acquired East London and also Selkent – which were adjacent but separated by the River Thames. London Regional Transport (or just London Transport as it had been calling itself) was replaced by a new body, London Transport Buses (LTB), with the responsibility for tendering routes, among other things. All routes would be tendered out by 2001 and contracts would be for five years at a time.

New firms joined in through the tendering process; indeed, LTB were actively encouraging smaller operators, but some familiar names like Grey-Green disappeared as large corporate groups emerged, taking in both the London Buses fleets and former National Bus Company fleets that had originally gone to management buy-outs. They also took over many of the independent companies. By 2000 names like Arriva, First Group and Stagecoach dominated bus operation both in London and nationally.

Another problem arose in that some of the smaller companies got into financial difficulties and went into receivership. Recruiting and retaining staff was a huge problem – some of the big national companies could get round this by bringing in spare staff from their provincial operations, particularly during the winter off-season.

LTB also began to adopt a more uniform policy with regard to liveries. In 1994 it was announced that purchasers of the London Buses companies would have to maintain an 80 per cent LT red livery for vehicles working in Central London (Zone 1), including the front of the bus. Existing companies with tendered routes in Central London, such as Grey-Green and London & Country, were permitted to keep their liveries on current contracts, but would have to adopt red on any new contracts won. Any new companies winning contracts into Zone 1 would also need to adopt the red policy.

At first the newly privatised London Buses fleets adopted their own variations on the traditional red livery – Metroline buses looked particularly smart with their blue skirts. Arriva, First Group and Stagecoach had all created a national livery scheme for their various fleets, none of which was red-based. First Group and Stagecoach adopted a red livery for London with flashes of other colours in their house style. Arriva adopted a red and cream variant of their national blue and cream livery, although some buses working wholly in the outer suburbs did receive the national scheme.

The new millennium coincided with a change in ownership for London's bus services. From 3 July 2000 a new mayor of London was appointed, who took over responsibility for London Bus Services Ltd and a new regulatory authority called Transport for London (TfL). The first London mayor was none other than Ken Livingstone, the former leader of the Greater London Council, under whose ownership fares had been subsidised until the 'Fares Fare' court challenge in 1982.

In 2002 it was decreed that all London bus routes should be worked by 80 per cent red buses, and not just those in Central London. Then, for contracts signed from 1 July 2004, TfL's livery policy was tightened to overall red, with only the fleetname to differentiate the separate companies. With this, London's almost twenty-year colourful era came to an end. Mind you, there were far fewer companies left by then, as most of the smaller companies had been bought out.

Some vehicles have since carried local route branding, commemorative liveries or special liveries for contract operations (e.g. for Kingston University), and, ironically, overall advertising, but otherwise red rules the day.

London Buses had withdrawn from many of the routes running to places outside Greater London since the cuts following the 'Fares Fare' ruling. These routes and those remaining that ran wholly or mostly outside the Greater London area were now tendered by their respective counties. This brought other new operators into 'red' border towns such as Romford and Staines, although of course some of these routes were won by companies also running LRT contracts. The London Buses subsidiaries and later privatised companies could also bid for these county contracts. These non-LRT or TfL contracts have not been restricted by the livery constraints in London, so now we have a situation where towns that were once predominantly 'red' like Loughton and Staines now see fewer or no 'red' routes running under TfL contracts, with those that do now not progressing further. However, there are always anomalies and in 2018, Romford, once very colourful, is now all 'red'. We also have TfL red buses once again serving Brentwood in Essex, as well as Thurrock Lakeside. Unfortunately, there is not enough space within this book to include all of these non-LRT contracts since 1985, with only a sample selection being shown.

Other Operators in 1985
Before Tendering

National Bus Company

Thames Valley had used double-deck buses on their routes from Reading to London for many years. Under the National Bus Company they were merged with Aldershot & District to form Alder Valley, only later to be split again into Alder Valley North and Alder Valley South. Both of these would use double-deck coach-seated buses on their routes from Reading, Bracknell or Aldershot to London. Alder Valley North later became the Berks Bucks Bus Co. (trading as Bee Line) and their Londonlink route passed to Reading Transport in October 1991. Alder Valley South ECW-bodied Leyland Olympian 1507 is at Hyde Park Corner on 1 April 1988, working route X8 to London Victoria.

Through London General, its main predecessor, London Transport had built up a substantial country area to the north and south of London, but not in the east. Here, Eastern National held sway, having the second largest presence in Romford. Routes from Southend came further west – the X12 (later 400) to Victoria or King's Cross, and the former City Coach Co. routes to Wood Green. From 15 June 1981 Eastern National route 251 from Southend was diverted to terminate at Walthamstow Central and the Wood Green garage was closed. A Leyland Olympian in the then current green and yellow livery loads there on 28 August 1986.

The new image for Green Line saw proper coach-bodied vehicles being used. DL4 was a 1981 Duple-bodied Leyland Leopard. It is seen at Heathrow Airport on 14 June 1984 on route 767. This was an express service from Victoria coach station to Heathrow, introduced in January 1982. The fair was £1.50, undercutting London Transport's slower Airbus service, which charged £2. You could also go by Piccadilly Line on the Underground, but not by British Rail – Heathrow was not connected to the main railway network until 1998.

Municipal Fleets: Reading and Southend

A consequence of the 1980 deregulation of long-distance services was the creation of a joint service between Reading and Southend by the two municipal fleets from the first day, 6 October 1980. From 16 January 1982 a London Transport Bus Agreement was granted, allowing for passengers to be carried for journeys wholly within the London Transport area. However, from 17 May the joint operation ended. Branded as 'London Express', Reading Leyland Titan 79 pauses at Hammersmith's long-gone Butterwick bus station on 26 April 1985. Reading was one of the few bus companies besides London Transport to buy the Titan.

In 1992, following a merging of Readings service with the Londonlink service acquired from Berks Bucks in October 1991, the route was rebranded as 'the London Line'. Leyland Olympian 83 in the new livery is passing St Paul's Cathedral en route to the Aldgate terminus on 27 March 1993. There appear to be no passengers on board. The service was withdrawn from May 2000.

Southend developed an extensive commuter service in the 1980s, acquiring many new and second-hand coaches. Most notable were the Van Hool Astromega double-deck coaches. C257 FHJ waits on the Green Park stand on 7 May 1986, along with one of the many Leyland coaches.

Coach-seated Leyland Olympian 265 lays over on Charing Cross Embankment before working a journey on the X1 to Southend on 5 August 1993. Southend Transport was sold to the British Bus group in June 1993, who were subsequently taken over by the Cowie Group (who were in turn renamed Arriva in 1998).

Leyland Olympian 447 was painted into this route-branded livery for the London services. Here it loads at Aldgate bus station on 27 May 1996.

A service also ran to London Victoria, which was marketed and liveried as part of the Green Line network. Former Southend 566, but by now Arriva 4331, was a Volvo B10M with Plaxton bodywork. It is seen departing from Basildon for London on 26 August 2000. This route passed to Stephensons in 2001 but was withdrawn in 2008.

Independent Companies

At the southern limits of LT red bus operation in the Croydon area, Banstead Coaches had a long-established route connecting Chipstead Valley with Banstead. On 27 March 1986 it was being worked by this Plaxton Derwent-bodied Bedford, which was bought new for the service. The route was later taken over by Epsom Coaches (see page 95).

Elms Coaches, Harrow, started running the abandoned section of LT route 98B North Harrow–Ruislip from 1 August 1966, between Ruislip and Rayners Lane station. In 1970 Elms merged with Starline Coaches and a new business, Elmtree Transport, was formed, operating from the former Starline premises in Wealdstone. Under the LRT Harrow Buses scheme, new route H13 duplicated much of the route, although Headstone Lane was only served by the 98B. However, LRT withdrew Elmtree's right to run the route and it ran for the last time on 22 January 1988. This Willowbrook-bodied Bedford YRQ came from Pangbourne Coaches in 1985 and is at Ruislip on 16 October 1986.

Under the LRT Harrow Buses scheme a new route, numbered 398, was licenced to Elmtree (t/a Scorpio Coaches), running between Ruislip and Northolt from 14 November 1987. SPK 115M, a Bristol LHS with an ECW body new to London Country, is seen on 13 October 1989. Scorpio, by now re-named Blue & White, gave up the operation at the end of 1996, and the route passed to Sovereign Bus from 2 January 1997.

Fountain Coaches bought the Feltham garage of Golden Miller (see below) along with their local bus routes. From April 1990, Fountain decided to cease their operation of route 600 Bedfont–Hanworth and 602 Feltham–Shepperton (Monday to Friday, peak hours). They passed to Westlink at short notice, who initially used Leyland Nationals. The 600 was replaced by new routes H24 and H25 later in the year, supported by Hounslow Council, and which were worked by London United (see page 52). RBW 83M, a coach-seated Bristol RE originally with the Oxford fleet, loads in Feltham on 19 March 1987.

F. G. Wilder started with one coach in 1955, but soon after bought the two coaches of Varney, Twickenham, keeping the fleetname Golden Miller (named after a racehorse, as Mr Varney had started his business with his winnings). Since 1967 they had started bus routes from Feltham to East Bedfont, Shepperton and Hanworth. From 1971, route 606 from Staines to Stanwell Moor was added. In December 1984 the company was bought by Tellings of Byfleet; then, in 1986, they moved into the Byfleet premises and the Feltham garage, along with the Feltham routes, was sold to Fountain Coaches. The two firms merged as Tellings-Golden Miller in 1987. A mix of new and second-hand vehicles was used, and here a Bristol RELL with an ECW body that was new to Hants & Dorset sets off from Feltham on 17 March 1986.

Down in South London, Guards of Caterham ran local route C4 between Coulsdon and The Mount. Seen on 27 March 1986, the route is being worked by a Ford A type minibus. This area would later be served by East Surrey's route 363 and London & Country's route 301, both using minibuses.

Metrobus was set up in 1983 when they acquired the Orpington-based Tillingbourne (Metropolitan) Ltd subsidiary of Tillingbourne. They had stepped in two years earlier following the collapse of Orpington & District and had in turn inherited routes started by North Downs in areas not served by LT. Services had developed into a pair of routes between Orpington and West Croydon (353/7), as well as route 354 Croydon–Bromley. This former West Riding Daimler Fleetline is seen on route 357 in Orpington on 17 July 1986.

New Bharat are an Asian-owned coach company from Southall, mainly serving the local Sikh community. Many of these work at Heathrow Airport and in July 1984 New Bharat introduced a route from Smith's Farm Estate, Northolt, directly to the airport and cargo centre. Journeys were timed to fit in with shift patterns at the airport. On 24 February 1985, this route-branded Plaxton-bodied Bedford coach leaves the airport bus station on the service.

By August 2001 the route had become 805, and this East Lancs-bodied Dennis Dart SLF bought new was in use at Hatton Cross station.

In May 1984 Victoria Shuttle Service Ltd started a route between Victoria railway station and the coach station for interchanging passengers and their luggage, with a fare of 20p. This was probably Britain's shortest bus route. It later ceased, but the route restarted in 1991, being worked commercially by R&I (see page 58). Victoria Shuttle used Dormobile-bodied Bedford minibuses and this example is seen in Eccleston Place, the arrival side of Victoria coach station, in 1984. Victoria library is behind the bus.

London Route Tendering From 1985

Contracts from 1985 to 1989

The first round of tendering saw two routes pass from London Buses to Eastern National, then still a part of the National Bus Company. Route 193 Romford–Emerson Park (County Hall Estate) transferred on 13 July 1985. Bristol VRs were used initially, such as 3100, seen at St Edwards Way, Romford, on 6 September 1985. All vehicles used on LRT contracts carried the LT roundel and a sign saying 'London Regional Transport Service'.

From the same date, 13 July, Eastern National also gained route W9 Enfield–Southgate. On this route a batch of Bedford YMQS vehicles with Wadham Stringer bodywork were used. The route was branded as the 'W Niner'. On 16 August 1985, 1057 pauses in the grounds of Highfields Hospital, Winchmore Hill, while en route to Enfield.

From 13 July 1985 London Country Bus Services (LCBS) gained route 313 Potters Bar–Chingford. Seen in Chingford on 11 July 1986, AN 323 is a former Strathclyde Leyland Atlantean with Alexander bodywork.

The other route gained by LCBS was the P4 Lewisham–Brixton, the closest route to Central London of those to pass into new hands. This was taken over from 3 August 1985. Leyland Nationals were used, and SNB 411 is at Lewisham on 6 September. The buses were based at the former Timpsons Coaches garage at Catford, which had been part of National Travel South East.

The first round also saw two routes passed to Independent operators. London Buslines, who were owned by Len Wright Travel, gained the 81 Hounslow–Slough. Ex-LT Daimler Fleetline GHV 33N pulls away from a stop on Bath Road, at the northern perimeter of Heathrow Airport, en route to Slough on 21 July 1985.

Route 146 Bromley North–Downe passed to Crystals of Dartford, who were a minibus operator with existing experience of bus work, having taken on route 858 Orpington–Biggin Hill from 26 May 1981 following the collapse of Orpington & District. A691 DMV, a Leyland Cub with Reeve Burgess twenty-nine-seat bodywork, is seen at Bromley North station on 30 August 1985. This route was lost on retendering in 1991.

Cityrama, a coach company involved in London sightseeing work, won the contract for route 200 from 22 March 1986. Ex-LT Fleetlines were used, such as GHM 813N, seen in Raynes Park on 16 March 1987. From 2 December 1988 the route reverted to London Buses, before then being worked by Kingston Buses, a 'low-cost' unit, who are not featured in this book as they retained the standard red livery.

The era of Eastern National Bristol VRs on the 193 did not last long. From 2 August 1986 the route was revised to incorporate the 256 and an express section was introduced between Romford and Hornchurch. Ford Transit minibuses took over and the route was branded as the 'Hornchurch Hoppa'. Eastern National had by now been privatised and a new livery adopted. It is seen at Romford on 14 August 1986.

Further rounds of tendering in 1986 saw Eastern National win routes in the Ilford and Walthamstow areas from 24 May. Seen at Ilford on 11 July, a Leyland National is working route 167 to Loughton station. Note the 'Citybus' branding applied to vehicles on London contracts.

Further routes passed to LCBS, including route 51 Woolwich–Orpington from 16 August 1986. On 28 August, Leyland Atlantean AN219 is seen in Orpington.

When London Country won route 268 Golders Green station–Finchley Road station, they equipped it with Mercedes-Benz L608D minibuses in a special livery and 'Hampstead Hoppa' branding. As such, MBM7 is seen at Golders Green on 10 July 1986.

From 31 May 1986 route 283 passed to ScanCoaches. New vehicles were acquired; namely, 12-metre-long Scania K92CRBs with Jonckheere Trans-City bodies – the first right-hand drive examples built. C354 SVV is seen at Hammersmith Butterwick on 13 June 1986. Note the unusual black on white blinds, which were not at all London standard. No other routes were won and the 283 reverted to London Buses in 1989.

Initially a dealer based at Grays and Hornchurch, Ensignbus moved to Purfleet in July 1981. They gained the contract to dispose of London Transport's unloved Daimler Fleetlines and in the 1980s they became a major player in London sightseeing work. Their involvement in LRT contracts started in June 1986 with route 145, and not surprisingly ex-LT Fleetlines were used. A second route, the 62, came in January 1987, being again worked by Fleetlines. Former DMS 2204 is seen in Barking on 3 April 1988.

The first of London Buses' low-cost units, Stanwell Buses (trading as Westlink) took over routes 116, 117 and 203 from 9 August 1986 using existing Leyland Nationals. While the basis of the livery was London red, white and blue bands were added. LS145, seen at Feltham on 12 March 1987, shows the original livery design, which was later modified.

Metrobus bought ex-London Fleetlines for their first tendered route, the 61, on which they started on 16 August 1986. Route 361 was a new Monday to Friday route worked by Metrobus from the same date. Seen at Bromley North station on 28 August was this Bedford YMT with Wadham Stringer bodywork – an unusual choice for London bus work.

Both new and second-hand vehicles would enter the fleet as further contracts were won. However, the first double-decker bought new, in 1985, was for their existing commercial route 357. Leyland Olympian C395 DML was working this route at Orpington on 17 July 1985 when seen. This bus has now been preserved. The 357 and commercial routes 353 and 354 were retained, becoming LRT-tendered routes in 1986.

A tendering scheme for the Orpington area in 1985 saw new local minibus routes R1–6 introduced from 16 August 1986. They were won by a new London Buses low-cost unit called Orpington Buses, trading as Roundabout, who adopted a maroon and grey livery. All of the Roundabout vehicles were new minibuses, but three different makes were used. RH4 was an Iveco with a Robin Hood body and is seen at Orpington on 28 August 1986.

At Orpington station on the same day is OV5 *Whirlwind*, an Optare City Pacer based on a Volkswagen chassis. The third type of vehicle, used later, was the longer MCW Metrorider, examples of which replaced Ivecos, which were then redeployed by Bexleybus. When new Dennis Dart vehicles were supplied to Selkent in 1990 for Roundabout services, these were in normal red livery with Roundabout fleetnames. In 1996 many of the Orpington routes were won on retendering by CentreWest, based in West London, who also took route 61 from Metrobus. Selkent's involvement and the Roundabout name both ended.

On 7 September 1986 London Country was split into four parts in preparation for privatisation. The parts were LCBS North East, North West, South East and South West. LCBS North East had routes 298 and 313, and gained route 359 (formerly route 259) from 25 October 1986. Atlantean AN72 is at Lower Edmonton on this route on 15 November 1986. However this was only a temporary contract – the route passed to Eastern National from 25 January 1987.

Each of the parts of LCBS adopted a new livery. The London Country North East version is seen on Leyland Olympian LR7 at Edgware on route 292 on 25 October 1987.

London Country North West started with routes 142 and 268. Leyland Olympian LR52 is seen at Stanmore on the former. Note the local brand name 'Watfordwide' above the entrance. 16 October 1986. This was later changed to 'Watford Bus'.

London Country South East was renamed Kentish Bus from 27 April 1987. Sporting its new fleetname, Atlantean EPH 224V departs from Woolwich for Orpington on 18 October. It is passing the entrance to Woolwich Arsenal station, whose buildings have since been replaced.

The fourth part of London Country was London Country South West. They started with six tendered routes won by LCBS in 1986. Others followed, including the 131 from 27 June 1987. This former Greater Manchester Atlantean is seen working the route at Kingston on 20 August 1987. London Country South West was sold to the Drawlane Group in February 1988.

The George Ewer Group (Grey-Green) was an established coach company. From 28 February 1987 they joined the ranks of tendered bus operators when they took over route 173. At first they traded under the name 'EastenderBus' and the vehicles were garaged at the former Dix Coaches premises at Becontree Heath. OKW 501R, seen at Beckton, is a DMS 'look-alike' Fleetline that came from South Yorkshire PTE.

A tendering scheme for the Harrow area saw another London Buses low-cost unit formed. Harrow Buses started on 14 November 1987 with a mix of new and second-hand vehicles and a red and cream livery was adopted. New minibus routes H11–H15 were worked by MCW Metrorider buses, such as E123 KYW, seen in Harrow on the first day.

Second-hand double-deckers came in the form of these Alexander-bodied Volvo Ailsas from West Midlands. V45 is seen with a Leyland National in Harrow bus station on 28 April 1990.

New vehicles were leased MCW Metrobus 2s. M1467 leads another Leyland National at Ruislip station on 26 March 1988.

As not all of the Metrobuses were in place for the start-up, ex-Greater Manchester Daimler Fleetlines were hired in the interim. GMPTE 7385 is in Harrow on the first day, 14 November 1987.

In July 1988 four Metroriders were hired from Northumbria while the local examples were having retarders fitted. 826 is seen in Harrow bus station.

When LRT announced the tendering of routes in the Woolwich/Bexley area, the Selkent district general manager negotiated a new low-cost unit working out of a reopened Bexleyheath garage. They won seventeen of the tendered routes with Boro'line taking the other routes. Eastbourne Corporation had an existing working relationship with Selkent and their blue and cream livery was chosen for the new Bexleybus operation. Bexleybus used a mixture of second-hand and new buses. Thirty-one ex-LT Daimler Fleetlines were sourced, of which fourteen were bought back from Clydeside Scottish. One-time DMS 1656 pulls away from General Gordon Place, Woolwich, on 19 February. The headquarters of the Woolwich Equitable Building Society provide the backdrop. The livery fell afoul of new LRT regulations in 1990, and as the Fleetlines were replaced by more modern Titans, most of these retained their red livery.

A batch of twenty-eight new Northern Counties-bodied Leyland Olympians was leased. L285 was in Thamesmead, working route 401, when photographed on 4 August 1990. When the routes came up for retendering in 1990, virtually everything was lost to other operators. Bexleyheath garage and many of the routes passed to London Central from 24 November 1990. The leased Leyland Olympians were returned to their dealer.

Single-deck vehicles comprised Leyland Nationals, ex-Roundabout Ivecos, MCW Metroriders and, later, Mercedes minibuses. This Optare StarRider with a Mercedes chassis approaches Kidbrooke on route B16 on 11 August 1989.

Boro'line was the trading name of Maidstone's municipal fleet. From 16 January 1988 they won four routes in the Bexleyheath and Eltham areas: 132, 228, 328 and 233. New vehicles to work these were not supplied in time, so vehicles were hired in from Hull and Greater Manchester. Hull 376, a Roe-bodied Leyland Atlantean, is at Bexleyheath on 17 January 1988.

A Northern Counties-bodied Atlantean from Greater Manchester, also in Bexleyheath on route 132, on 8 February 1988.

A batch of Leyland Olympians with Optare bodywork was delivered in February 1988 for these routes. A pair are seen at Eltham station on 9 March 1990.

When Grey-Green gained routes in North London in 1987, they reverted to their own fleetname while retaining the brown/white/orange livery. New vehicles were also bought, such as this Scania, seen at Southgate on route 125 on 23 March 1988.

Routes 298 and 313 had been with London Country North East, but following an employee strike the contracts were transferred to Grey-Green from 22 February 1988. At first vehicles from the coach fleet were used, until buses could be sourced. Duple-bodied Leyland FYX 812W was on duty in Potters Bar on 9 March 1988.

Borehamwood Travel Service (BTS) worked route 292 during the strike by LCBS-NE and were then awarded the route. They also had Hertfordshire-contracted services in their home town. Leyland Atlantean MUA 863P was in Elstree on 6 March 1989.

Atlas Bus was the trading name for Pan Atlas Leisure, London. They gained their first London tender from 30 July 1988 with route 112, later gaining route 107 as well. Leyland Lynx E299 OMG stands outside the classic Charles Holden-designed architecture of Arnos Grove station on 8 March 1989. It will travel round the North Circular Road all the way to Ealing Broadway.

Frontrunner was a subsidiary of East Midland Buses from Chesterfield, and from 24 September 1988 gained London routes 248 and 252. Former Greater Manchester Leyland Atlanteans were the vehicles acquired for the routes, and the livery was the same as that used by the parent fleet. They also gained a number of Essex contracts, which took their vehicles into Brentwood and Loughton. Atlantean JVM 989N is seen in Romford on 21 October 1988. The Frontrunner regime did not last long, as from 30 June 1989 the London routes passed to Ensignbus, following the Stagecoach Group's acquisition of East Midland and their withdrawal from the contracts.

A new route introduced on 19 November 1988 was the P14, linking the Isle of Dogs with Surrey Quays (a redevelopment of the former Surrey Docks, the only docks south of the river). The route ran via Rotherhithe Tunnel, which had not been served by buses since 1968. Only minibuses could work through the tunnel and the contract was awarded to Kentish Bus, who provided MCW Metroriders in this route-branded livery. F861 LCU leaves Surrey Quays on 24 December 1988.

A major coup happened when Grey-Green were awarded trunk route 24 Highgate–Pimlico from 5 November 1988, the first tendered route through the heart of Central London. New Volvo Citybuses were bought with Alexander bodies, and by now a livery more appropriate to the company's name had been adopted. 144 is in Stag Place, Victoria, on 26 March 1989. The company were taken over by the Cowie Group in 1991.

From 19 November 1988, Boro'line won route 188 Greenwich–Euston station, taking them into Central London. Once again new vehicles were not delivered in time and vehicles needed to be hired; this time, Ipswich and Nottingham came to the rescue. Ipswich Roe-bodied Atlantean 1 stands at Euston on 18 December 1988.

Nottingham Atlantean 202 makes an unusual sight crossing Waterloo Bridge on 7 February 1989.

The vehicles purchased for the 188 were Volvo Citybuses with Alexander bodies. A pair of these are on the stand outside the Royal Naval College at Greenwich on 13 April 1989.

From 26 November 1988 routes 422 and 492 had their contracts transferred from Bexleybus to Boro'line. NSP 319R was a Volvo Ailsa with an Alexander body, which was formerly with Tayside until acquired for the 492. It is pulling away from the stands at Bexleyheath on 15 March 1989 when seen.

To work the 422, Leyland Nationals were bought from London Buses. While these were being prepared, others were hired from London Country North East and Eastbourne Corporation. Eastbourne 20, itself former London Transport LS309, is at Bexleyheath on 15 March 1989.

Suttonbus was another London Buses low-cost unit, which commenced from 26 November 1988. The livery was basically red, but a mushroom skirt was applied rather than the usual grey. Fleetlines were the main vehicles used except for some Metroriders on new route 352. DM2589, seen arriving at West Croydon bus station on route 154 on 16 August 1989, also had a yellow between-decks band, others having none.

From 30 March 1989 a newcomer on the scene was Docklands Transit, whose routes mainly radiated from the Isle of Dogs. Some routes served roads not served by LRT routes and routes were operated on a Hail and Ride basis. The vehicles were Mellor-bodied Ford Transits. The company was part of the Transit Holdings Group, the product of a management buyout of Devon General from the National Bus Company. Docklands Transit was run as a commercial venture with fixed term licences issued by the Traffic Commissioner, not as London-tendered routes, and London bus passes and Travelcards were not accepted. This led to its downfall and the commercial routes ceased in November 1990. E210 BDV is at the Isle of Dogs Asda store on 13 April 1989.

The C4 was a minibus service between Putney Pier and Chelsea Harbour that was introduced initially for a six-month experimental period on 1 April 1989. It was supported financially by Hammersmith & Fulham Council. It was worked by London Buslines and Mercedes-Benz G644 YVS is seen near Putney Bridge station on 9 August 1990. The route was retained, although it passed to Thorpes in 1995.

From 27 April 1989 London Country South West was renamed as London & Country to reflect its increasing role in LRT-tendered operations. A new livery was also devised. G621 BPH, an East Lancs-bodied Volvo Citybus, is at Twickenham on route 110 on 17 March 1990, a route worked since January 1987.

Westlink route H20 was a new route developed in partnership with Hounslow Council in 1989. Three wheelchair-accessible CVE Omni buses were employed, one in Westlink colours and two in this white Hounslow livery. F265 WDC is seen attending a bus rally at Southsea in June 1989.

From 19 August 1989, cross-river route 108 passed to Boro'line. This was (and still is) the only route to traverse Blackwall Tunnel. Only single-deck vehicles could be used because of clearances in the tunnel and as a result Leyland Lynx buses were bought. 807 is at Lewisham bus station on 8 May 1990.

Atlas Bus gained route 107 from 7 October 1989. A Leyland Olympian with Northern Counties bodywork, G761 UYT works a journey in Queensbury on 13 October 1989. Both this and route 112 were lost on retendering in 1994.

R&I of Park Royal won the tender for route 268 from London Country North West from 3 June 1989. Iveco minibuses were bought. F206 HGN is at Golders Green station on 27 June.

R&I won new route H17 from 2 September 1989. LCY 299X, a Bedford YMQS with Lex B37F bodywork, is at Sudbury on 28 April 1990. These vehicles were acquired from Tillingbourne, but were new to South Wales.

E964 PME was one of a pair of Optare-bodied Leyland Olympians that were surplus to the order placed by Boro'line. Here it is seen at Norwood Junction on 13 April 1989 on Cityrama's other route, the 196. This was awarded from 7 February 1987 and passed to London & Country from 28 October 1989. The Olympians were then converted to open-top for sightseeing work.

Contracts from 1990 to 1999

Kentish Bus expanded beyond their south-eastern territory in 1990 when they won the contract for routes 22A, 22B and 55, linking the Hackney area with Central London – all north of the Thames and going nowhere near Kent! New Leyland Olympians with Northern Counties bodies were bought for these routes. This example is seen at Hackney on 8 March 1990 and shows the Kentish bus livery.

By the early 1990s, there were parts of suburban London where the number of tendered routes exceeded those still worked by London Buses' red vehicles. Bexleyheath was one such location and here we see two Kentish Bus vehicles, two from Boro'line and one Titan from London Buses Selkent. The date is 28 February 1991.

Transcity Link, Sidcup, won route B15 from Bexleybus when the Bexley area routes went to tender again in 1990. Route 286 was later added. However, the routes and vehicles were taken over by Kentish Bus from 29 October 1993, bringing this operator's time on LRT contracts to an end. The tri-axle Talbot Pullman was an unusual type to be found on London-tendered services, but Transcity Link bought five for route B15, as seen at Bexleyheath on 28 February 1991. They later also ran Darts on route 286.

Later vehicles for Harrow Buses, in the shape of Mercedes-Benz/Optare StarRiders delivered in 1989, were in a more standard style red livery. The Harrow routes came up for tender again in 1990, and on this occasion only routes 183, H12/4/5 and new route H18 were retained. These routes now came under Metroline, using the Harrow Buses fleetname. The leased MCW Metrobus 2s were returned to their dealer.

In January 1989, following privatisation and sale to the AJS Group, London Country North East was split into County Bus in the east and Sovereign in the west. Sovereign adopted a blue and cream livery. They won routes in the Harrow area when these came up for retender, and Mercedes-Benz minibus H929 FGS is seen at Harrow bus station on 13 March 1991. This part of Sovereign later traded as Sovereign Harrow.

London Country North West adopted this green and grey livery in 1989, seen to advantage on Carlyle-bodied Dennis Dart DC4. Seen on 13 March 1991, this is at Harrow bus station on route 258, which was previously with Harrow Buses.

In April 1990 Eastern National was acquired by the Badgerline Group. From 29 July 1990 they were split up, with the southern section becoming Thamesway. This included all the LRT tenders. Thamesway adopted a new livery, which is seen on Leyland Olympian 1002 at New Barnet, working route 307 on 9 April 1991. The route, formed from part of the 107, had been won by ENOC from 27 September 1986.

The new London & Country fleetname was certainly more appropriate when the company gained routes through Central London, such as the 176 in 1990. Leyland Atlantean XPG 192T crosses Waterloo Bridge en route for Penge on 30 December 1990.

When London & Country gained routes 78 and 176, vehicles were not available to take up the routes at first, so the company hired in vehicles from South Yorkshire Transport. 1710, a Roe-bodied Leyland Atlantean, is passing the Horniman Museum, Forest Hill, on route 78 on 18 November 1990. Note the 'On hire to London & Country' label in the nearside window.

Some of the other vehicles on hire from South Yorkshire Transport carried the Sheffield Mainline livery, as does 1691, seen outside the Elephant & Castle shopping centre on the same day.

Armchair of Brentford's first LRT contract came in 1990, for route 260 Shepherd's Bush Green–North Finchley. By 1998 they were running seventy-four buses, all bought new, plus a coach fleet. They would work route 65 until June 2002, when it passed to London United. Leyland Olympian H562 GKX is at Petersham on the route on 14 April 1991.

Capital Citybus was created when Ensignbus sold their London contracts, vehicles and Dagenham depot to CNT Holdings of Hong Kong in December 1990. Vehicles originally ran as Ensign Citybus in the former Ensignbus blue and silver livery. Alexander-bodied Leyland Olympian 123 is at Chingford station on 9 November 1991.

An interim livery applied to a few vehicles featured yellow rather than blue with the silver characteristic of Ensignbus. One such recipient was MCW Metrobus 2 282, seen at Romford on 2 November 1991.

The Capital Citybus livery was yellow with red stripes, as used in Hong Kong. 170 was a MCW Metrobus 2 which had started out in the Harrow Buses fleet (see page 30). On 26 May 1992 it was pictured near Crossharbour station on the Isle of Dogs, working route D6.

In the later revised livery style, Westlink DWL1, a Wrights-bodied Dennis Dart, passes through Petersham on route 371 on 14 April 1991. This route was interesting in that it included a section via Kingston Hill that had previously been worked by an independent operator, Continental Pioneer. They had served this road following LT's withdrawal of route 235 in 1966, until LT diverted route 71 to reincorporate the route in September 1980.

An initiative funded by Hounslow Council saw routes H24 and H25 worked by wheelchair lift equipped Iveco minibuses in this livery and branded as Hounslow Hoppa. London United FR3 is at Hatton Cross station on 21 May 1991. These routes had replaced Fountain Coaches' route 600, which had been surrendered in 1990 (see page 14).

The later style livery of London Buslines is carried by G50 XLO, an Alexander-bodied Leyland Olympian bought new. It is seen at Hatton Cross station, working route 90 on 19 August 1991.

On hire to London Buslines on 19 August 1991 was this South Yorkshire Transport Renault. It was noted at Hatton Cross with a somewhat makeshift blind in place.

Golden Miller had run services before 1985 (see page 15). They were bought by Tellings of Byfleet, the fleet moving into the Byfleet depot in 1986 and merging in 1987. They then became part of the Drawlane Group in 1990. As TGM Buses they won their first London contract when they won an amended route 116 and route 117 from Stanwell Buses (Westlink) in 1991. Leyland National TOF 713S is at Feltham on 19 August 1991.

From 15 February 1992 the Boro'line operations of Maidstone all passed to Kentish Bus, while the Maidstone services were put into administration, later passing to Maidstone & District on 1 June. Volvo Citybus 927 has had a Kentish Bus transfer applied somewhat untidily over the former name when photographed in Woolwich on 9 March 1992.

London Coaches was the London Buses operating unit for the sightseeing and tours business. On 29 February 1992 they also took on tendered bus services when they won former Green Line route 726 from Dartford to Heathrow Airport. Three months later they were the first London Buses unit to be privatised, going to a management buyout. DAF SB220 buses with Ikarus bodies were obtained. J807 KHD is at Heathrow on 8 March 1992. The route and vehicles would later pass to Capital Connections.

Grey-Green bought a variety of different vehicles for bus work, but also recycled some of their existing coaches. Most unusual were these Volvo B10 coaches, which were re-bodied as double-deck buses in 1992. Note the long wheelbase and short rear overhang on 166, seen at Moorgate on 24 March 1992.

Javelin Coaches were awarded the mobility bus network for the Kingston and Richmond area from April 1992. Four Mercedes-Benz 709D minibuses were used with seventeen seats plus space for three wheelchairs. Seatbelts were also fitted. J514 WTW stands with a sister vehicle at Kingston on 2 October 1992.

The eastern part of London Country North East had become County Bus in 1989, with a new livery. County Bus also used local fleetnames for each garage. At Chingford station on 1 April 1992, a Reeve Burgess-bodied Dennis Dart displays the name 'Lea Valley' as it waits to work a 444 journey to Turnpike Lane station. County Bus would pass to the Cowie Group in 1996.

R&I Dennis Dart with Carlyle bodywork photographed at Hammersmith Butterwick on 5 April 1992. The 391 was worked by R&I on Sundays only. This location has since been completely redeveloped.

Thamesway was part of the Badgerline Group, hence the badger emblem on this Plaxton-bodied Dennis Dart. It is seen in London Wall, close to the Liverpool Street station terminus of route 214, on 23 August 1992.

R&I restarted the Victoria Shuttle from 1991, using one of their Ivecos in a dedicated livery. Appropriately registered RIB 4316, the bus awaits custom at Victoria station on 8 May 1993. This service was ended after R&I's takeover in 1995.

From 24 April 1993 Kentish Bus won another route out of Kent when they took on route 19 Finsbury Park–Battersea Bridge, along with their allocation of twenty-four RMLs, which they leased. This was the first crew-worked route awarded to a private company. The RMLs received the Kentish Bus livery, and very smart they looked too, with route details and no advertising. RML 2452 is at Hyde Park Corner on 30 April 1993. Sunday services were OPO using the Olympians from the Hackney routes.

London Suburban Bus was the trading name for GENSAM Holdings, who traded in Liverpool as Liverbus. They won contracts for route 4 Archway–Waterloo and 271 Liverpool Street–Highgate from London Northern from September 1993. They also gained night route N6. On 12 April 1995 London Suburban Bus were taken over by MTL, the purchasers of London Northern upon privatisation. The company was initially kept as a separate entity but LT red livery was adopted for both fleets. Ex-LT Leyland Titan 501 is at Archway on route 4 on 17 October 1993.

Displaying the name of the parent Liverpool-based company is 104, a Northern Counties-bodied Volvo. It was pulling out of Finsbury Square, Moorgate, on a journey to Highgate Village on 30 September 1993. This bus was in use pending delivery of new vehicles.

In December 1993 BTS became the second company to take over a Routemaster-operated route when it took on route 13 with twenty-two leased RMLs. Unusually, unlike the other Routemaster-operated routes in London, the company also ran on Sundays, until July 1996, when OPO buses took over on the Sabbath. BTS was bought by the Blazefield Group in 1994, who renamed the business London Sovereign. RML 2674 is at Trafalgar Square on 12 February 1994.

Route 52 was awarded to London Coaches in December 1993, along with a new night-time variant – the N52. They bought the London operations from Atlas Bus in October 1994 when their contracts ended and moved route 52 to the Atlas garage in Harlesden, thus saving on dead mileage. Route 52 also now ran with Atlas Bus fleetnames. Former London Transport Titans were bought and T438 is at Hyde Park Corner on 24 June 1994.

Now running with an Atlas Bus fleetname, T399 stops at Hyde Park Corner on 18 August 1994. In early 1995 the business, route 52 and the Titans were sold on to Metroline, who repainted them into their fleet livery.

A livery variation that wasn't to be! In 1994 Capital Citybus acquired five Roe-bodied Leyland DAB articulated buses from British Airways, registered RLN 233–6/8W. This one was exhibited at the North Weald bus rally, painted in the fleet livery with Red Arrow branding and blinds in anticipation for bidding for the contract for Red Arrow services 507 and 521. However, the contract was retained by London General, the existing operator.

This Renault minibus of London Buslines was working a Mobility Bus contract when seen at the Brent Cross Shopping Centre on 4 October 1994.

In a later 'more red' livery, R&I Dennis Dart 241 departs from Brent Cross Shopping Centre on 4 October 1994. On 24 October 1995 the company was acquired by MTL London Northern, who absorbed both the buses and coaches under their own name.

From 1 January 1995 the London operations of London & Country, with garages at Croydon, Walworth and Dunton Green, were separated under a new Londonlinks fleetname. This Alexander-bodied Volvo Citybus, new to Boro'line, was passing through Russell Square on route 188 to Greenwich on 28 March 1997 when seen.

In April 1995 the Badgerline companies merged with the GRT Bus Group to become First Group. Displaying a new livery and First logo, a Thamesway Dennis Dart passes through Enfield on route 191 to Edmonton Green station on 4 May 1996.

London Country North West was bought by Luton & District in October 1990, who introduced this blue/yellow/grey livery, and changed their name to The Shires in 1995. Olympian 5021 waits to depart Watford Junction station for Brent Cross on route 142 on 2 April 1997. Luton & District would later become Arriva The Shires.

In 1995 Kentish Bus adopted a new green and yellow livery. This ex-Northumbria Leyland Olympian shows the new style, which was originally intended to be for commercially operated routes only. It is passing the grounds of Woolwich Arsenal on route 96 to Dartford, one of their few LRT-tendered routes that actually did reach into the administrative county of Kent! This route had previously been with Bexleybus. Under Cowie ownership, the Kentish Bus London operations were transferred to Cowie Leaside or South London in 1997.

Frank E. Thorpe & Sons took over the inter-station Carelink service from London General on 24 October 1992. It was relaunched as Stationlink with additional stops, including Victoria coach station. However, this only ran hourly and in one direction around the loop of stations. Initially Mercedes-Benz 709Ds were used with fourteen seats, a chairlift and space for two wheelchairs. In 1996 the Stationlink service was revamped with new vehicles, the frequency being doubled, and a service provided in both directions. Optare Excel N100 FET works the SL1 service at King's Cross on 13 July 1996 when seen. The livery style emphasises the low-floor accessibility credentials of the bus. The SL1/SL2 would eventually be partially replaced by new, conventional bus route 205 Paddington–Whitechapel in August 2002.

When route 105 was won by London & Country in April 1996, the Plaxton-bodied Dennis Darts used thereon were given route branding. They were operated from a separate outstation in Greenford, where they quickly became somewhat scruffy. Then, from 23 November, the route and buses were transferred to CentreWest, who operated the route from Alperton garage. DSL30 is seen at Southall on 5 November 1996.

Route 285 was another of the routes serving Heathrow Airport. Route branding was applied when London Buslines gained the route. Dennis Dart 614 is seen at Feltham station with another of the company's buses behind on 6 July 1996.

Crystals made a comeback when they were awarded the R2 and R7 in a retendering of Orpington routes in 1996. Mercedes-Benz N601 JGP typifies the new vehicles. Crystals would be bought by TGM in 2003, but this isolated area of their operation was sold on to Metrobus (by then part of Go-Ahead) in 2005.

Thorpes' MCW Metrorider E137 SNY is seen near Putney Bridge station on route C4 on 17 August 1996. This route had been won from London Buslines in 1995. It would eventually be replaced by new route 424 in April 2001, worked by London General.

Limebourne were owned by Q Drive, who were also the owners of London Buslines when it was bought by CentreWest. London Buslines had been intended to be the operator of route C10 in 1996, working it from the Limebourne garage. However, as Limebourne were not bought by CentreWest, they took the route themselves. An Optare Metrorider demonstrator passes the former BOAC air terminal opposite Victoria coach station on 16 June 1996. Limebourne bought similar vehicles, which were required to have an 80 per cent red livery.

Route branding was applied by Metrobus for new buses on route 358 Bromley North–Crystal Palace, a route that needs to have single-deck vehicles because of a low bridge at Shortlands station. Optare Excel P510 DUG is seen in a more rural setting at Green Street Green on 14 December 1996.

Sovereign took over Borehamwood Travel (BTS), who won the tender for Routemaster-operated route 13, taking over the existing vehicles. The Routemasters retained their existing colours with a change of fleetname. RML 2569 passes through Trafalgar Square on 15 February 1997. The RMLs remained until August 2001, when, following the contract being re-awarded, they were replaced by reacquired and refurbished RMs in standard red.

When Capital Citybus won route 91 Crouch End–Trafalgar Square, Metroline Leyland Titans that had previously been with London Coaches for route 52 were put to work, in their existing liveries, until new vehicles were delivered. 957 passes through Russell Square on 29 March 1997.

A red and yellow livery was adopted to comply with LRT Zone 1 requirements when route 91 was won. Dennis Dominator 268 is at King's Cross station on the route on 2 April 1997. Note the unusual position of the fleetname – presumably so that it will not be obscured by advertising.

Docklands Transit returned to the fold in 1993, being awarded the contracts for routes 287, 366 and 368. These routes still traded as Docklands Minibus, although none of them actually touched Docklands. In 1996 they gained route 106, which was worked by Dennis Darts. On 22 July 1997 Docklands Transit was purchased by Stagecoach Holdings and the routes were transferred to Stagecoach East London. Dennis Dart 426 is at Hackney on 26 August 1997.

Harris Bus was a subsidiary of Frank Harris (Coaches) Ltd, Grays. Local bus operation began in April 1986 and the company won a number of contracts for routes in the Grays Thurrock area from London Country in October 1986. Route 108 through Blackwall Tunnel was the first LTB contract from April 1997. Other routes south of the Thames followed, and further contracts were gained in the Ilford area in 1997. Optare Excel R378 DJN carries Eltham Link branding for route 132 when seen at Eltham on 20 March 1998.

Harris Bus East Lancs-bodied Leyland Olympian 359 is seen in Romford, 3 November 1999.

When the Ilford area routes were gained, not all the vehicles were delivered in time for the take-up of the services, so some vehicles were hired from Ipswich in the meantime. 22, a Roe-bodied Leyland Atlantean, is on the 129 when seen on 19 July 1997. A Docklands Transit Mercedes-Benz can be seen behind.

A route-branded livery style for Limebourne on this Plaxton-bodied Dart, which is seen at Wimbledon on the 156 on 21 October 1997.

In 1997 the London operations of Kentish Bus were transferred to Cowie Leaside and South London. Cowie changed their name to Arriva and phased out the former company names in favour of a national brand identity and livery. Formerly Kentish Bus, Arriva L558 YCU, a Northern Counties-bodied Leyland Olympian, pauses in Sidcup en route to Bromley North station. Note the local strapline 'Serving Kent Thameside', which was used on vehicles in south-east London, Dartford and Gravesend. 8 July 1998.

Armchair P29 MLE, a Plaxton-bodied Dennis Dart, in Hounslow on route 117 on 16 August 1998.

In 1998 Capital Citybus were bought by First Group, who ran them as a separate division – First Capital. All vehicles, depots and contracts were transferred, with the business continuing under its existing management. The red and yellow livery used on central area buses was adopted as standard throughout. FirstGroup had been unsuccessful in the original London Buses privatisation but had subsequently bought CentreWest, who also owned London Buslines in 1997. This Marshall-bodied Dennis Dart displays the livery style applied by First Group in London. It is at the Crossharbour terminus on the Isle of Dogs on 9 October 1999.

West Midlands had had a presence in London when they bought Westlink in 1994, the first of the London Buses subsidiaries to be privatised, but they sold it on to London United in 1995. They returned to the fold in 1998, trading as Travel London and winning routes 211 and C1 from London General. A 9.6-metre Optare Excel on route 211 stands in Buckingham Palace Road, Victoria, on 5 July 1998.

On hire from parent company Travel West Midlands, this Wrights-bodied Volvo B6 is seen at the Victoria station forecourt on 30 June 1998.

Capital Logistics was formed from a merger of Capital Coaches and Whytes Airport Services, both of Heathrow. They won route 726 from London Coaches in June 1998, along with the vehicles used on it, later winning route U3 as well. Optare Excel R990 EWU was in Uxbridge on route U3 on 20 October 1998.

Thorpes applied their red and yellow livery in a variety of different ways to the Dennis Darts used when they won route 210. This was arguably the most extreme style! S532 JLM leaves Golders Green station on 10 October 1998. Thorpes would become one of the more enduring independents, being taken over by Metroline in 2004.

Major problems happened when Capital Logistics won the contract for route 60 Old Coulsdon–Streatham Common in 1998. As was the norm now, new buses were specified, but the Plaxton and Optare-bodied DAFs were not ready in time. Selkent and Blue Triangle provided buses at first, but Selkent's were needed for new contracts at Bexleyheath in January 1999. The contract was then transferred to a new operator, Driver Express/Omnibus London, who said it would hire buses until the new DAFs arrived. At the last minute it was able to supply only one bus, so for a while the service came to be operated by vehicles and drivers from a number of different companies, up to five a day. Consequently, Capital Logistics were given the contract back and eventually some of the new buses came in March. The one bus provided by Driver Express/Omnibus London, an ex-Reading Transport MCW Metrobus, still in its original colours, is at Streatham on 26 January 1999.

Among the companies providing vehicles for route 60 was Classic Coaches of High Wycombe with a Leyland National. That's a lot of dead mileage involved to get there! It is seen at Streatham on 2 February.

On 20 February, Nostalgiabus of Mitcham was running a very smart RM 1571, complete with a full set of blinds.

T134 AUA, one of the Capital Logistics Plaxton-bodied DAFs, is seen at Purley on 13 April 1999. No fleetname has been applied as Plaxton did not know who was going to be the eventual owner! Capital Logistics was bought out by Tellings Golden Miller later in 1999, with both companies becoming part of the new Status Group.

Q Drive, the owner of Limebourne, went into receivership in October 1998. The management bought the business in November, but the buses were leased and the lessors immediately reclaimed the vehicles. Other operators stepped in to provide a stopgap service until Limebourne were able to buy eleven early Darts (dating from 1990–1) from Metroline, as they were surplus. One of these, H142 MOB with Carlyle body, pulls away from Victoria station on 28 March 1999.

T402 LGP was a Caetano-bodied Dart bought new. It is at Wimbledon on route 156 on 26 March 1999 when seen.

Vehicles of Rainham-based bus company Blue Triangle were a common sight in East London on rail replacement work, and they also worked tendered services for Essex County Council, including routes that ran into Romford. However, in 1999 they gained their first London Buses-tendered route when they were awarded new route 474 from Beckton to Canning Town via North Woolwich and London City Airport. At first Metrobuses were used, either in the red and cream fleet livery as here, or in a new, mostly red version. MCW 462 (originally M462) is at North Woolwich on 4 May 1999.

Epsom Buses route 598 (see page 95) was merged with ex-London Buses route 166 to run hourly from West Croydon to Epsom. Unusually, the route was shared with Arriva London South, who ran two buses an hour from West Croydon to Caterham, providing a twenty-minute frequency over this section. This Epsom Buses Alexander-bodied Dart is at Purley on 1 June 1999. The contract became all Arriva in July 2001.

In 1999 route 292 came into the hands of Sovereign. This smart route-branded Volvo Olympian with Northern Counties bodywork is at Colindale on 5 June. The company had become part of the Blazefield Group and the livery was similar to that used by other Blazefield companies, such as Yorkshire Coastliner. The original tender for the 292 had been with BTS. Blazefield sold Sovereign (London) to London United in November 2002, who have retained the Sovereign name but not the livery.

After Ensignbus sold their London-tendered operations to Capital Citybus, they concentrated on sightseeing services under the London Pride name. However, in 1998 they regained a licence for bus work and started commercial operations in Essex from their base at Purfleet. The success of the Lakeside Shopping Centre at Thurrock in 1990 and the opening of Bluewater across the Thames at Greenhithe in 1999 gave them the opportunity to develop routes to serve these, including routes 324 and 348 to Romford, where this ex-Greater Manchester MCW Metrobus was found on 3 November 1999. The 324 had been started by Ensignbus and had passed to Capital Citybus, but when they became First Capital they withdrew from the Essex commercial routes.

London Traveller was mainly doing school services and rail replacement work until they won LTB tenders in 1999. The Yorkshire Traction Group bought a 25 per cent stake in Metropolitan Omnibus (London), a new company set up to operate London contracts and schools work under the London Traveller name, and moved into the former Scan Coaches depot in Harlesden. Seen here at the Showbus rally at Duxford Airfield on 26 September 1999, London Traveller V514 EFR was a Volvo B6BLE with East Lancs bodywork.

East Lancs-bodied Volvo W516 CCK arrives at Willesden Junction station on 28 August 2002. Later that year Metropolitan Omnibus sold out to Thorpes.

Mitcham Belle was a long-established coach operator who gained their first tender with route 127 in 1999. Dennis Dart W124 WGT is at Raynes Park on 19 June 2000.

Wings of Uxbridge was an established coach operator which was awarded new route U7, a replacement for former route 207A, from November 1999. East Lancs-bodied Dennis Dart is seen in Uxbridge on 11 March 2000.

Contracts from 2000 to 2005

Epsom Buses won a number of routes in the Sutton area, such as S3, on which this short Alexander-bodied Dart is seen on 8 April 2000.

Connex was a subsidiary of the French utilities and transport company CGEA. It already had a UK rail franchise for routes from London to parts of Kent and Sussex, but it was also awarded route 3 Oxford Circus–Crystal Palace from 2000. Their trains ran in a yellow and cream livery, but running through Central London was a 'red' route. Other routes were later added. Connex sold out to National Express in February 2004, who brought back the Travel London name used earlier, until the two routes then operated had passed to Limebourne, who were later taken over by Connex. Alexander-bodied Dennis Trident TA26 was in Whitehall on 5 March 2000 when seen.

Limebourne took over running route G1 from Arriva London South in 2000 due to staff shortages. Dennis Dart H129 THE displays the red and cream Central London variant of Arriva colours at Clapham Junction on 30 August 2000.

East Thames Buses was set up by London Transport Buses from 25 March 2000 to take over from Harris Bus after they went into receivership and no other buyer came forward. The Belvedere local council base was retained for the operations south of the Thames, and the former LT Ash Grove garage was reopened for the Ilford routes. Standard red livery was quickly applied to the fleet. Olympian 346 passes Valentines Park, Ilford, on 22 April 2001.

When route H50 was awarded to Wings in 2000, the buses were given this promotional 'trainlink' livery. W438 CRN is at Hayes station on 27 March 2003. Wings were bought by TGM in 2004.

New low-floor vehicles for Blue Triangle comprised two batches of Dennis Tridents with East Lancs bodywork. These sported an 80 per cent red livery, as shown by DL921 in Romford on 10 November 2001.

London Easylink was the trading name of Durham Travel Services, who took on route 185 Victoria–Lewisham from 13 February 2001. In 2002 they also gained route 42, but on 21 August 2002 the company went into receivership. Plaxton-bodied Volvo B7TL X185 FBB pulls out of the Lewisham station forecourt, past the entrance to the Docklands Light Railway, on 25 February.

Limebourne lost the contract for route C10 in April 2001, and Blue Triangle stepped in on a temporary basis until London Central assumed operation in September. Mercedes-Benz Varios were used in a mixture of red, white or, as seen here on 26 April, blue. Limebourne sold out to Connex on 7 July 2001.

Hackney Community Transport, trading as CT Plus, made their debut by winning a contract for the Enfield/Hackney mobility bus network in 1999. They then gained route 153 in 2001 and have gained further routes since then. They operate out of part of the Ash Grove garage, which was also used by East Thames Buses and now Arriva. As of the time of writing, in 2018, they remain one of the largest TfL contract operators not part of one of the big national groups. The company started when the 80 per cent red livery policy was already in place, but even the side yellow flashes would become unacceptable in due course. This is an East Lancs-bodied Dennis Trident, one of the first double-deckers supplied for new route 388 in 2003.

Route 394 'Shoreditch Hoppa' started in September 2001, a half-hourly mainly hail-and-ride service, part supported by the Shoreditch New Deal Trust. It was worked by Hackney Community Transport with a pair of blue Rohill-bodied Renaults. With no blinds, only a paper route number and the TfL sticker below the windscreen, there is very little to suggest that this vehicle is working a London bus route. This later became a conventional route worked by red buses.

Acquired from London & Country and retaining their livery, TGM Dennis Dart P294 FPK is at Hatton Cross station on 11 May 2001 when seen. Route 490 had been acquired from CentreWest in exchange for the U3 in April.

Another Dennis Dart and an Optare Excel load at Richmond on 30 July 2001.

In 2001 Epsom Buses changed their trading name for London-tendered work to Quality Line and adopted a plain red livery. This Dennis Dart, seen at Wallington on 9 February 2002, displays the new order of things. However, Epsom Buses continue to run local bus services under their own name and colours in Epsom.

With the edict in 2002 that an 80 per cent red livery should be the basis for all contracted London buses, the later style of 'more red' livery is shown by Mitcham Belle Caetano-bodied Dart KU02 YBG at New Malden, 14 August 2002. In 2004 Mitcham Belle were bought by Centra – the bus division of Central Parking Systems.

Docklands Transit's operations were sold to Stagecoach in 1997, but they retained a base for contract work and returned to London bus work in 2002, having been awarded route 167. New Caetano-bodied Dart SLF HV02 PDO is at Loughton, 17 July 2002.

Seen at Victoria station on 10 September 2002, an Arriva Metrobus from their Original London Sightseeing Tour subsidiary helps out on route 185 following the collapse of London Easylink, who went into receivership on 21 August and were immediately closed down without any prior warning to TfL. They had replaced some of the other operators who had initially stepped in after the collapse, but had to pull out because of school bus commitments when the new term started.

When the requirement for a mostly red-based livery came in, Metrobus adopted this style, with a red base but featuring their traditional blue and yellow. From 3 September 1999 Metrobus had been part of the Go-Ahead Group; however, in line with that group's ethos, the separate Metrobus identity and livery were retained. Scania 459 runs beneath the tram wires in Addiscombe Road, Croydon, on route 64 on 28 May 2003.

The 'more red' livery, as applied by TGM on this Caetano-bodied Dart, seen at Feltham on 15 March 2003. On the next year's new buses the white roof became red too. However, in June 2005 the London and Surrey-tendered services, along with 182 buses, were bought by National Express to be merged with their Travel London business.

In the later 80 per cent red livery, Armchair DT4, an Alexander-bodied Dennis Trident, loads at Brentford on 6 August 2003. Armchair succumbed to takeover by Metroline in November 2004.

A new attempt at providing the Victoria coach station–Victoria station shuttle was started by DB Transport in 2004 with a pair of Optare Metroriders and L192 DDW is seen at the coach station stop. This was not TfL sponsored, so Travelcards were not accepted and a red livery not required. It only lasted until July 2004.

Ealing Community Transport joined the ranks of London-tendered bus operators from April 2003 with route 195. KX03 HZF was a Caetano-bodied Dennis Dart, and was photographed at Hanwell on 13 June 2005. This was their interpretation of 80 per cent red.

As the livery restrictions tightened, the blue/yellow band on Metrobus vehicles became thinner. Scania YN53 RXK was in Bromley High Street on 3 May 2005 when seen.

A new name in London was Centra (Central Parking Systems), who bought Mitcham Belle in 2004. Caetano-bodied Dennis Dart DC20 is in Wimbledon town centre on route 493 on 31 May 2005 when seen. It has had a repaint and is now all red. The colourful days were over.

National Car Parks took over the 33 and 419 from London United in late 2005. As a latecomer to tendering, NCP Challenger was restricted to an all-red livery. SN55 HKF crosses the railway bridge at Barnes station on 17 June 2006.

County Route Tendering
From 1985 (Selection)

East Surrey operated a number of Kent and Surrey CC contracts, the latter of which included routes into Croydon. UGB 14R, a second-hand AEC Reliance with Duple bodywork, is seen in Croydon on their route 301 on 30 July 1993.

Epsom Buses' Plaxton-bodied Bedford YMT D602 RGJ stands outside Fairfield Halls, Croydon, ready to work back to its home town. The 598 was a Surrey CC-tendered route, taking over and extending the old Banstead Coaches route from Chipstead Valley to Banstead (see page 13). It was later incorporated into London-tendered route 166 (see page 79).

Sampsons of Hoddesdon won three ex-LT routes in the Waltham Cross area from 24 May 1986 on Essex tenders, including the 250 to Loughton. Leyland Nationals were also used. The routes passed to Frontrunner in 1988. Ex-London DMS 1762 is at Loughton station on 11 July.

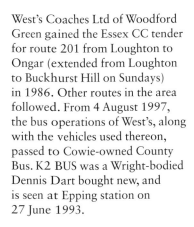

West's Coaches Ltd of Woodford Green gained the Essex CC tender for route 201 from Loughton to Ongar (extended from Loughton to Buckhurst Hill on Sundays) in 1986. Other routes in the area followed. From 4 August 1997, the bus operations of West's, along with the vehicles used thereon, passed to Cowie-owned County Bus. K2 BUS was a Wright-bodied Dennis Dart bought new, and is seen at Epping station on 27 June 1993.

Bibliography

Baker, Michael H. C., *London Transport Since 1933* (Shepperton: Ian Allen, 2000).

Buses (Hersham: Ian Allen, monthly from 1985+).

King, Nicholas, *London Bus Handbook Part 1: London Buses Ltd* (Harrow Weald: Capital Transport, various editions 1990s).

King, Nicholas, *London Bus Handbook Part 2: Independents* (Harrow Weald: Capital Transport, various editions 1987/1990s).

McLachan, Tom, *London Buses 1985–1995: Managing the Change* (Glossop: Venture, 1996).

Reed, John, *London Buses Past and Present* (Harrow Weald: Capital Transport, 1988).

Wallis, Philip, *London Transport Connections 1945–1985* (Harrow Weald: Capital Transport, 2003).

Wharmby, Matthew and Rixon, Geoff, *Routemaster Omnibus* (Hersham: Ian Allen, 2008).

Various publications, including fleet lists and newsletters by the London Omnibus Traction Society, have also been referenced. This is the principal society for enthusiasts of London Transport and its successors, and anyone with an interest in the London bus scene past and present is recommended to join. www.lots.org.uk.